source **to** resource

FROM
FIELD
TO
PLATE

MICHAEL BRIGHT

WAYLAND

www.waylandbooks.co.uk

Contents

Essential food 3

Eat up! 4

Food origins 6

In the field 8

On the farm 10

Intensive farming 12

Organic farming 14

Fresh foods 16

Preserving food 18

Friendly bugs 20

Food in shops 22

Preparing food 24

Safe food 26

World food 28

Glossary 30

Further information 31

Index 32

Field with wheat crop

Packaging

Transporting

Essential food

At one time, the distance from field to plate was no more than a few miles. People bought food from **local markets** or shops, which were supplied by nearby **farms**; and they could only get food that was **in season**. Nowadays, people can buy **exotic** foods from distant lands and eat familiar foods out of season. Food is **traded** across the world, so now the distance between field and plate can be many thousands of miles.

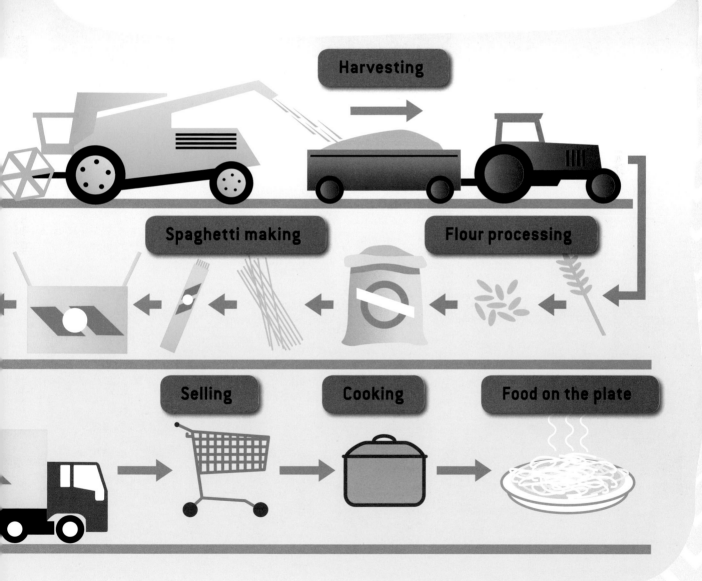

Harvesting

Spaghetti making

Flour processing

Selling

Cooking

Food on the plate

Eat up!

Food is anything we eat that provides our bodies with essential 'nutrients'. These are the goodness in foods that includes fats, proteins, carbohydrates, minerals and vitamins. From food we get energy for the body to work and grow.

A bit of everything

Humans are known as 'omnivores'. Our early human ancestors got their food by hunting animals and collecting plants and fungi. These hunter-gatherers had to eat whatever was to hand, which means our bodies even today are designed to eat and digest food from both plants and animals.

Plants only

Some people choose not to be omnivores: they prefer to eat just plants, algae and fungi, and nothing else. They are called 'vegans' and 'vegetarians'. Some vegetarians might also eat eggs and dairy products, such as cheese and yoghurt, but neither vegans nor vegetarians eat meat.

A variety of good wholesome foods is essential for a healthy life.

Poppadoms, meatballs and noodles

The kinds of food we eat most are usually determined by where we come from. Chinese food is very different from Indian food that, in turn, is different from Scandinavian food. However, the food industry today has become so international that people can eat all these foods, at any time, in many cities around the world.

The right colour

The colour of food was important to our ancient ancestors. The colour of fruit, for example, told them when it was ripe and ready to eat. Purple or green moulds on food indicated it was rotting and inedible.

More recently, scientists wanted to see if this still affects the way we look at foods today. They coloured foods like freshly baked bread with purple, blue and green edible dyes, and took them to market. Nobody would eat them!

The blue-grey patches are a fungus called mould. It shows this bread is not safe to eat.

Food origins

Our earliest ancestors hunted wild animals and collected the tastiest plants, but it soon became clear that they could get more food, and more easily, if they looked after animals and controlled how plants grew. This was the start of agriculture, and the beginning of the journey from field to plate.

Tracing food origins

Many foods we eat every day have ancient origins. To find out when and where they first occurred, scientists study their chemical DNA. It is in every living cell, and carries the instructions for what a plant or animal will be like and how it will grow. DNA also gives us an idea of what modern foods' ancestors were like. It can tell us when and where people grew the first crops and reared the first animals, and it is surprisingly precise.

Wild cattle

Ferocious wild cattle, known as the aurochs, were once scattered all over Europe and Asia; they were powerful and dangerous. These cattle were tamed by a brave farmer just once on an ancient farm in what is now Iran. All of today's cows can be traced back to this single herd of just 80 animals that lived about 10,500 years ago.

Ancient people were wary of wild bison and aurochs: the aurochs were tamed, the bison were not.

The ears of rice bend over with the weight of the ripening grains.

Wild rice

Rice was one of the earliest crops to be cultivated. Today, all varieties grown come from a wild species of rice found in the valley of the Pearl River in southern China between 8,200 and 13,500 years ago. Today, rice feeds many of the world's people.

Wild potatoes

Almost every variety of potato we grow today originally came from a type of wild potato that grew on the islands of the Chiloé Archipelago, off the coast of south-central Chile. It was brought to Europe by Spanish explorers in 1562, first to the Canary Islands and later to mainland Europe.

Wild fowl

The red jungle fowl of India and Pakistan is the ancestor of all the chickens in Europe, the Americas, the Middle East and Africa today. The ancient Egyptians called it 'the bird that gives birth every day'. Asian chickens have a different jungle fowl ancestor.

In the field

Farmers who grow crops are called arable farmers. They might grow wheat, barley or oats – in fact, just about any plant that we eat. The farmer's year is an exhausting non-stop cycle of preparing the ground, planting, growing and harvesting, and it is very dependent on the weather.

Ancient crop

Barley was one of the earliest cereal crops grown by ancient peoples 10,000 years ago. It is easy to recognise because each grain of barley has a long spike, called an awn, growing out of it.

Barley likes cool conditions and can grow in nutrient-poor soils, unlike wheat.

Grain harvesting

A combine harvester is used to harvest barley, wheat and other cereal crops. It 'reaps' or cuts the crop, 'threshes' it to loosen the grain from the husks and leaves and then 'winnows' it to separate the grains from the rest of the plant. The stems and leaves, known as straw, are thrown out to be collected later, while the grain is poured into a truck to be transported away and turned into foods, such as bread.

The barley grower's year

This is what a typical year might look like for an arable farmer growing spring barley in Europe.

FEBRUARY

Time to plough the ground. The plough turns and loosens the soil, buries the stalks from last year's crop and prepares the soil for planting.

Drilling is the sowing of seeds in rows with a tractor and drill. The drill ensures that the seeds drop on to the ground at an even rate so they are not too close together or too wide apart.

Flat metal rollers are then towed behind the tractor to firm up the seedbed, break up bits of soil and reduce attacks by slugs.

MARCH

The crop starts to shoot up with the longer days of early spring. The first fertiliser is put on the field to help the crop to grow.

MAY

A battle rages in late spring. It's between weeds and barley, each competing for the goodness in the soil and for living space. Farmers help the barley by spraying a chemical, called a herbicide. It does not affect the barley but it kills the weeds.

JUNE

Damp and dreary weather can cause leaf rust and powdery mildew that kill barley leaves. These crop diseases are caused by fungi, so the farmer sprays the crop with fungicide to kill them.

AUGUST

The sun is shining and it is harvest time. Barley grain is transported away to be turned into bread, beer and other foods. Straw is used for winter bedding for farm animals. Stalks, or 'stubble', are left in the field until ploughing begins next year.

On the farm

Farmers who look after cows, sheep, pigs and chickens are livestock or pastoral farmers. Like the arable farmers, they have a yearly cycle during which they raise their animals. Some also grow their own animal feed for the winter.

🍽 Cattle farming

Dairy farmers breed cows for milk, while beef farmers rear their cattle mainly for meat. Different breeds of cattle are reared to produce different farm products. For example, German black-and-white Friesian cows are kept for the large quantities of milk they produce, and the Japanese black wagyu is bred for high quality beef.

Friesian dairy cows produce the most milk.

Kangaroo meat is strong in flavour and low in fat.

DID YOU KNOW?

While Australia is the natural home for kangaroos, increasingly people in other countries are rearing them for meat to eat! The same is true for ostriches from Africa, water buffalo from Asia, alpacas and llamas from South America and reindeer from Scandinavia.

The shepherd's year

Shepherds keep sheep, with different breeds of sheep suited to different landscapes. This is a year in the life of a British sheep farmer.

October/November

Ewes (female sheep) graze on rich pastures. This ensures they gain weight and are in good condition before being introduced to the rams (male sheep) for mating - or 'tupping' as it is known by shepherds.

March/April

Lambing time, when lambs are born. The lambs feed on their mother's milk, play and grow.

December/January/February

Ewes feed on poorer quality pasture through the winter, and may be given hay if the snow is deep.

May/June

The lambs are encouraged to stop drinking their mother's milk and eat grass instead. Adult sheep are sheared to remove their fleeces before the hot weather. Early-born lambs go to market.

July/August/September

Ewes are given a medicine to rid them of parasitic worms, and sprayed with chemicals to get rid of fly maggots. Late-born lambs go to market for sale.

The sheep's fleece is shorn in May or June and may be used to make woollen clothes and carpets.

Intensive farming

Traditional farming gives nature a helping hand with fertilisers and pesticides, but intensive farming takes this even further. Large numbers of animals can be packed together to maximise the use of space, and large quantities of crops can be grown, even out of season.

Battery hens

Chickens are sometimes reared in row upon row of small cages. They have little room to move so simply sit, eat and lay eggs. Many countries have banned this kind of factory farming, but there are still some that produce almost all their eggs this way.

Pigpens

Like chickens, some pigs are also reared indoors rather than being able to live outside, as wild pigs would. Female pigs who are pregnant are put into 'sow stalls'. These are barely wider than the pig, so it cannot turn around. When it is time to give birth, the mother pig is put in a 'farrowing stall'. Here, she can lie down to suckle her piglets, but they are kept separate from her at other times. It prevents her from rolling over and squashing them, but she has little room to move. The practice is banned in the UK and New Zealand.

Only female hens are kept in battery cages for their eggs. Males are killed immediately after hatching.

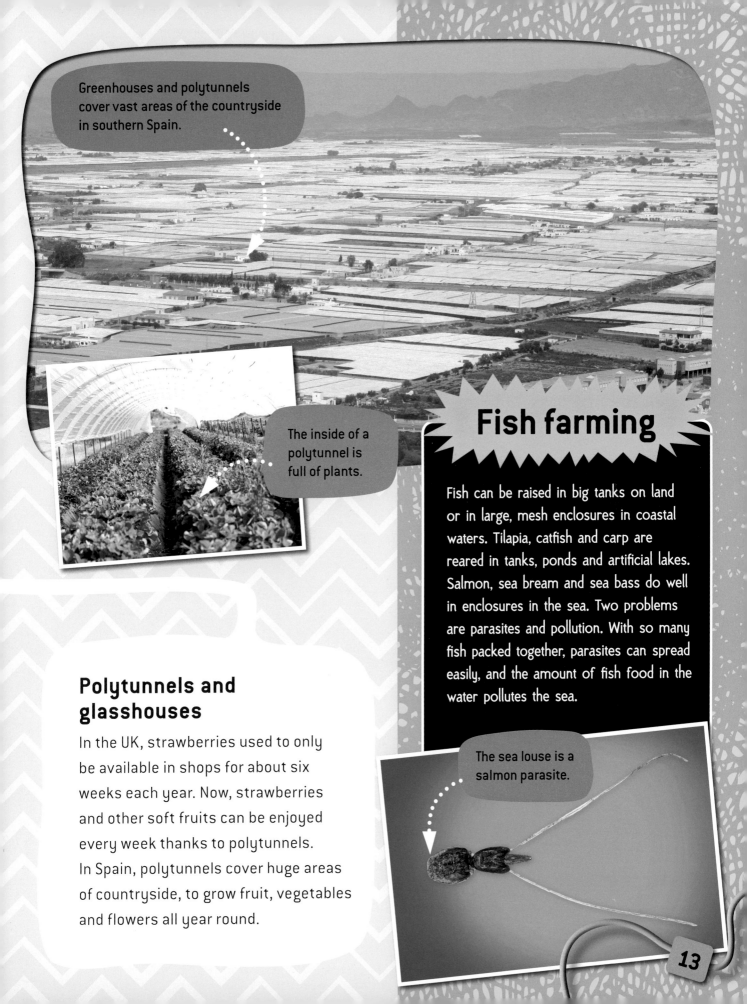

Greenhouses and polytunnels cover vast areas of the countryside in southern Spain.

The inside of a polytunnel is full of plants.

Fish farming

Fish can be raised in big tanks on land or in large, mesh enclosures in coastal waters. Tilapia, catfish and carp are reared in tanks, ponds and artificial lakes. Salmon, sea bream and sea bass do well in enclosures in the sea. Two problems are parasites and pollution. With so many fish packed together, parasites can spread easily, and the amount of fish food in the water pollutes the sea.

The sea louse is a salmon parasite.

Polytunnels and glasshouses

In the UK, strawberries used to only be available in shops for about six weeks each year. Now, strawberries and other soft fruits can be enjoyed every week thanks to polytunnels. In Spain, polytunnels cover huge areas of countryside, to grow fruit, vegetables and flowers all year round.

Organic farming

Organic farming is very different to intensive farming. No chemical fertilisers or pesticides are used to grow crops, and livestock must have access to pastures. In many countries, only farmers with a certificate from farm inspectors can claim their produce is organic.

Crop rotation

Organic farmers use traditional ways of farming that have changed very little through the centuries. Crop rotation is at the centre of organic farming. This is when different crops are planted in a field each year to keep the soil fertile. One crop can benefit the next one. If the same crop was planted each year, pests would build up and nutrients in the soil would get used up. Crop rotation breaks the life cycles of pests and diseases.

A crop rotation sequence for a single field could be wheat, clover to increase nutrients, maize and then fallow for the field to recover.

Resting fields

Part of the crop rotation cycle is to leave some fields fallow, meaning they are ploughed but not seeded. This allows the soil to recover. Alternatively, fields can be planted with special plants, such as clover, which add nutrients to the soil. In this way, the soil remains rich and fertile.

YEAR 4: FALLOW

YEAR 1: WHEAT

YEAR 3: MAIZE

YEAR 2: CLOVER

Free range pigs do what pigs like to do – snuffle about and forage for food.

Promoting growth and stopping pests

Organic farmers spread animal manure and compost on fields, as natural fertilisers, to boost plant growth. Local wildlife, such as insects, spiders and birds, is encouraged to feed on pests as a form of natural pest control. It does not always work, so if pests do get out of control, certain pesticides made from natural sources may be used.

Happy animals

Livestock on organic farms is free range. Animals live in fields when the weather is good, but have shelter during bad weather. Free range cattle, sheep, pigs and chickens appear to have less stress and therefore less disease, so they need less medicine.

Organic pros and cons

PROS

- Natural habitats and wildlife are less affected by organic farming.
- The soil tends to be in better condition.
- Organic food is said by experts to be healthier, safer and tastier.

CONS

- Insect pests and weeds have more impact.
- Some natural pesticides based on the chemical copper can be harmful.
- Crop yield is reduced.

Fresh foods

Transport plays a vital role in getting food from the field to your plate. Some produce, such as grain, can be stored for a long time. However, most foods, such as fruit, vegetables and fish, need to be transported quickly before they go bad. Livestock needs to be taken to the abattoir with as little stress to the animals as possible.

Livestock to market

Shepherds use sheepdogs to herd their flocks down from the hills, and cattle are rounded up and put into pens. From here, they are loaded on to trucks or railway cars and taken to the abattoir to be killed.

Machine or hand-picked

Most crops are dug up or picked using mechanical harvesters. There are machines that shake fruit trees, dig up potatoes and other root vegetables, and even one that 'hulls' rice – it separates the husk from rice grains. However, some crops, such as the grapes for Burgundy wines, vanilla pods from orchids and saffron from crocus flowers, are still harvested by hand.

In Europe, strict laws ensure farm animals are transported without injury and unnecessary suffering.

A constant temperature can be maintained inside a refrigerated shipping container.

Fishing

Freshly caught fish is packed with ice to keep it fresh until the boats return home. At the quayside fish market, some is sold to local fishmongers and restaurants. The rest is loaded into refrigerated vans and trucks and sent to central fish markets, such as Billingsgate in London or Fulton in New York. From here, it is distributed to supermarkets, shops and restaurants around the country.

International transport

Some crops, such as bananas, only grow in tropical places. Hot countries can also grow crops all year round, so they supply produce out of season to countries with cooler climates. This means fruit and vegetables are transported around the world, usually in refrigerated ships, aircraft and shipping containers. Cooling slows down the natural ripening process. The food is then fast-tracked through ports and airports.

Fresh fish have clear eyes and bright red gills.

Preserving food

Not all food is delivered fresh. For centuries, people have developed all kinds of ways to preserve food so that it can be stored for longer. Some food can even be processed naturally to change it into something that has a nicer taste or more goodness in it.

Freezing

Freezing prevents chemicals in foods, called enzymes, from working. The cold stops or slows the ripening and rotting process. Many foods are sold as frozen products, such as fish fingers and frozen peas.

Drying

Removing water slows the growth of bacteria in food so it does not rot. It is a method of preservation that can be traced back to at least 12,000 BCE. Fish, meat, fruit and vegetables can all be dried.

Salting and pickling

Edible salt is used to salt foods, and salty water or brine can pickle foods. Most bacteria die in salt. Two of the oldest-known salted foods are salted fish, such as dried and salted cod, and salt-cured meat, such as bacon.

Sugaring

Adding sugar to foods also kills bacteria. The process is used to turn fruits into jams, jellies and marmalades, and to preserve vegetables such as ginger.

Canning

Food is processed, such as by boiling, to kill bacteria, and is then sealed in an airtight container. It can last a long time – in 1974, cans of food from a ship that sunk in the Missouri River in 1875 were tested. The food did not look good, but there was no bacterial growth and it was considered fit to eat!

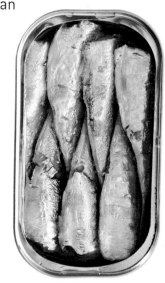

Smoking

Exposing food to wood smoke is a very old way of preserving it. The process dries the food, and chemicals in the smoke help to preserve it by killing bacteria. It also adds a nice taste to foods, such as smoked fish and smoked hams.

Space food

Astronauts rely on freeze-dried food. Freezing food rapidly and placing it in a vacuum preserves it. It can then be kept in a tube so it doesn't float away. Instant coffee and dried fruits in breakfast cereals are also preserved in this way.

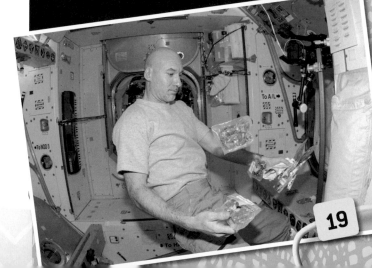

Friendly bugs

Bacteria and fungi might seem to be enemies of the food industry, since they are part of the rotting process of food. Yet, bacteria and a type of fungus called yeast are also used to preserve and process foods, such as in bread- and cheese-making.

Daily bread

Bread is probably the oldest man-made food. There is evidence of bread-making by prehistoric people 30,000 years ago in southern Europe. They made simple flatbreads from crushed grains mixed into a paste with water, then cooked them over a camp fire.

Modern bread is similarly made from flour and water, but with the addition of yeast. When mixed together they produce dough. When the dough is left to rest, the yeast causes the sugars and starches in the flour to ferment, producing carbon dioxide. This lightens the dough before it is baked.

Bread rolls are made with the help of yeast.

Blue cheese has blue veins made by mould.

Nectar of the gods

To brew beer, wheat or barley is mixed with water and yeast, whilst crushed grapes or other fruits are added to yeast to make wine. The starch in grain and the sugars in grapes are broken down and turned into alcohol by the yeast. Brewing is thought to have originated in ancient Mesopotamia (now Iraq) in 9,500 BCE, making it the earliest alcoholic drink. The earliest record we have about wine is from 6,000 BCE in Georgia, on the border between eastern Europe and Asia.

Say cheese

The earliest-known cheese-making occurred 7,500 years ago in Poland. Cheese is made from cow, goat, sheep or buffalo milk, with the help of bacterias that occur naturally in the milk or are added artificially. Rennet, an enzyme from the stomach of cattle, is added, which separates the bacteria-modified milk into curds and whey. The whey is drained away and used to make foods such as whey butter, and the curd is used to make the cheese. Each type of cheese is prepared in a slightly different way. Blue cheeses, for example, have the Penicillium mould added to give the cheese its blue spots and veins.

Food in shops

Food from farms, fishing boats, bakeries and cheese-makers eventually finds its way to shops, supermarkets and restaurants. Speed is of the essence because the food must reach its destination before it goes off.

Farm to supermarket

Supermarket chains buy some of their products directly from farmers, who they trust to supply them with the best produce. The sale is held at large distribution centres, along with foods from all over the world, before being transported by road to the individual shops.

Specialist food markets

Produce is also collected together at special 'wholesale' markets, such as the fruit and vegetable market at New Covent Garden and the meat market at Smithfield, both in London, UK. There, shop and restaurant owners bid for the best produce, before it is delivered to their businesses.

An indoor market in Asia.

Many of the fruit and vegetables in a supermarket are a uniform size, shape and colour.

Fruit and vegetables at a greengrocer can be all shapes and sizes, including 'wonky' ones.

Specialist food shops

While supermarkets tend to stock just about everything you need at home, smaller shops specialise in particular foods. Here are a few:

- **Grocery stores** stock mostly 'dry' goods, such as breakfast cereals and tinned food.

- **Greengrocers** sell fruit and vegetables.

- **Butchers** sell meat, poultry and eggs.

- **Fishmongers** sell fish and shellfish.

- **Bakeries** make and sell foods based on flour, such as bread, cakes, pastries and pies.

- **Delicatessens** sell specialist and luxury foods, especially foods that are not normally available in general food shops and supermarkets.

The best cuts

Many foods arrive at shops in packaging, but inside the package, most foods have changed little in appearance from when they left the farm. Meat is different. A carcass of beef, lamb or pork must be sliced into smaller pieces. Butchers in different countries cut up meat in different ways, and they give each piece its own special name. In the UK, for example, the rib-eye steak is a cut of beef from the rib section of the cow. It is known as a Scotch fillet in Australia, entrecôte in France and a Delmonico steak in New York.

23

Preparing food

The last stage of the journey from field to plate is in the kitchen. Some foods are eaten raw, while others are cooked using heat. Cooking food helps to break it down, making it easier to digest and to release more nutrients.

 There are several basic techniques used in modern cooking.

Boiling cooks food in boiling water or in other water-based liquids, such as milk or stock. A gentle boiling is called simmering. If the liquid moves without forming bubbles it is called poaching.

Frying is to cook food in oils or fats. They can be animal fats, such as lard or butter, or plant oils, such as olive oil and rapeseed oil. It is a type of cooking that started in ancient Egypt in about 2,500 BCE.

Grilling uses dry heat, sometimes from an open fire, that cooks food on one side at a time. The food can be on an open wire grill or in a grill pan with raised ridges.

BOILING

FRYING

GRILLING

Baking uses dry heat in an oven to cook breads, cakes and pastries. Heat travels from the surface of the food to the inside, so the outside is often a dry crust, while the centre is soft.

Roasting uses dry heat, usually in an oven. Very hot air, at a temperature of at least 150 °C, surrounds the food and cooks it evenly.

Steaming relies on water boiling continuously to form steam. The steam envelops the food and cooks it. Some people think it is the healthiest way to cook foods because vegetables and meats keep their nutrients. Some nutrients are lost in other forms of cooking.

A zillion-dollar lobster frittata

Food can be fun, but also pricey. The world's most expensive omelette is found at Norma's Restaurant in New York. It is lobster on a bed of fried potatoes covered with egg and topped with expensive Sevruga caviar. The supersize frittata costs about $1,000!

BAKING

STEAMING

ROASTING

Safe food

Food is the perfect place for bacteria to grow. The bacteria in food can cause food poisoning, or the food can carry other diseases, such as typhoid, from one person to another. The World Health Organisation has noted five key ways to help keep food safe.

1. Keep clean

• Dangerous microbes are carried on hands, wiping cloths, cooking pots and pans, and cutting boards. They can easily be transferred to food.

• Wash your hands before handling food.

• Wash cooking equipment and surfaces.

• Protect kitchen areas from insect pests and other animals.

2. Separate raw and cooked

• Raw animal products, such as meat, poultry and seafood, and their juices, can carry microbes that contaminate other foods.

• Separate raw meat, poultry and seafood from other foods.

• Use separate knives and cutting boards for preparing raw foods.

• Store food in containers to avoid contact between raw and prepared foods.

3. Cook thoroughly

• Proper cooking, to a temperature of at least 70 °C, kills most dangerous microbes.

• Cook food thoroughly, especially meat, poultry, eggs and seafood.

• Bring soups and stews to boiling.

• After cooking, make sure the juices of meat and poultry run clear, not pink.

Chicken is fully cooked when its juices run clear.

A kitchen must be cleaned after the preparation of every meal or diseases can be spread.

4. Store food at safe temperatures

- Microbes reproduce rapidly in foods stored at room temperature, and some will still grow in the fridge.

- Do not leave cooked food at room temperature for more than two hours.

- Put cooked and perishable food in the fridge quickly, but do not store it there for too long.

- Keep cooked food piping hot, at more than 60 °C, before serving.

5. Use safe water and foods

- Some uncooked foods can be contaminated with microbes, and damaged or mouldy raw foods can contain dangerous chemicals.

- Use clean drinking water and select fresh foods.

- Choose foods that have been made safe, such as pasteurised milk.

- Wash fruit and vegetables, especially if eaten raw.

World food

Global food consumption is generally on the rise, with more people in developing countries having access to adequate food supplies. Even so, at least 165 million children around the world do not have enough food to stay healthy.

The wrong foods

Having more food does not necessarily mean a healthier life. In many countries, diets have changed to include more processed foods, such as takeaway fast foods and ready meals, with high levels of fats and sugars. This has led to obesity and a higher incidence of dangerous diseases, such as heart disease and diabetes.

Food waste

It may come as surprise to learn that over 30 per cent of food in developed countries, such as the USA, is wasted. That is about four times the amount of food imported by poorer developing nations in Africa.

Fast and convenience foods tend to have high levels of salt that cause dangerously high blood pressure in people.

Households are very wasteful. One in three bags of food shopping goes straight in the bin and off to the landfill site.

Saving seeds

As an insurance policy against diseases wiping out the crops we grow today, the seeds from the world's plant species and ancient crop varieties are stored in special seed banks. The largest are the Millenium Seed Bank, near London, UK and the Svalbard Global Seed Vault in Norway. They both house billions of seeds in underground vaults that would survive a nuclear war or similar disaster.

Loss of food varieties

Three-quarters of the world's food is obtained from only 12 plants — such as rice, maize and wheat — and five animal species: cows, sheep, pigs, goats and chickens. Many farmers have replaced their local varieties of crops with fewer high-yield varieties. Ancient breeds of farm animals have been lost in favour of the few that provide more meat. If diseases hit these modern crops and farm animals, the world would have little left to eat. Fortunately, some farmers are trying to preserve the old breeds and grow the old crops, so the future for food looks bright.

This is the Svalbard Global Seed Vault in Arctic Norway.

Glossary

abattoir A place where animals are slaughtered

ancestor A person who lived before you, to whom you are related

bacteria Microscopic living things, some of which can cause disease

carbohydrates Nutrients that include sugars and starches

compost A mixture of dead plant material that has rotted and broken down, which is used to improve the quality of soil

contaminated Unclean

cultivate To prepare and use land for crops

cured Describes food preserved by salting, drying or smoking

diabetes A disease associated with eating too much sugar

enzyme A chemical produced by living things that helps chemical reactions to take place, such as the digestion of food

fallow Describes a piece of land that has been ploughed and left to rest

fats Solidified animal or plant oil

fermentation A chemical reaction caused by microscopic living things, such as yeasts, that converts sugar to carbon dioxide and alcohol

fertile Describes something able to produce crops in large quantities

fertiliser A chemical that makes the soil more productive

fungus Part of a group of plant-like living things that includes mushrooms, toadstools, moulds and yeasts

graze To feed on grass or other low-growing plants

husk The outer covering of seeds, such as rice grains

intensive farming The production of crops with artificial fertilisers and pesticides. Or, the cramming of animals together and keeping them healthy with medicines.

microbe A microscopic living thing, for example, bacteria that can cause disease

mineral A chemical in food that is essential for healthy living

mould A fungus that causes the furry growth on rotting food. Some food, such as blue cheeses, have mould added to it for taste.

nutrient A chemical from food that is needed by your body to stay healthy

obesity An excess of bodyweight caused by eating unhealthy foods

pasteurised milk Milk that has been exposed to high temperatures to reduce the number of dangerous microbes

perishable Describes something that rots quickly

pollution Chemicals that are harmful to living things

poppadom A thin, round, crispy Indian bread

protein An essential chemical in food, such as meat, fish and beans, that is important in growth and the repair of tissues

species Types of plant or animal that are closely related and can breed together

starch A common nutrient found in the stems, roots, fruits and seeds of plants, such as corn, potatoes, wheat and rice

stubble Short, stiff stalks of straw that remain on a field after harvesting

synthetic Describes something that is not of natural origin

traditional Describes something that has been done the same way for many years

vitamins A group of substances that are essential in healthy diets

yield To produce or provide something, such as a crop

Further information

BOOKS

Farming: Changing Times
by Ruth Thomson, Franklin Watts 2004

Food Safety and Farming: In the News
by A Smith, Franklin Watts 2002

From Farm to Table: Food and Farming
by Richard and Louise Spilsbury, Wayland 2010

Sustainable Farming: How Can We Save Our World?
by Carol Ballard, Franklin Watts 2009

WEBSITES

Visit this website for fun facts about where food comes from:
http://www.foodafactoflife.org.uk/site.aspx?siteId=15&t=2

The BBC Bitesize webpage will give you lots of information about food and farming:
http://www.bbc.co.uk/education/topics/z672pv4/resources/1

More facts about food and farming:
http://www.myfarmfood.co.uk/manchester/farming/

Index

agriculture 6

animal 4, 6, 9–10, 12, 15–16, 24, 26, 29

bacteria 18–21, 26

bakery 22–23

butcher 23

crop 6–9, 12, 14–17, 29

farm 3, 6, 8–11, 14–16, 22–23, 29

farmer 6, 8–10, 12, 14–15, 22, 29

fertiliser 9, 14–15

fish farming 13

fishing 17

fishmonger 17, 23

fungi 4–5, 9, 20

greengrocer 23

grocery store 23

harvest 3, 8, 9, 16

intensive farming 12–13

livestock 10, 14–16

market 3, 5, 11, 16–17, 22

mould 5, 21, 27

organic farming 14–15

pesticide 12, 14, 15

plant 4, 6, 8, 13–15, 24, 29

preserving 18–19, 20, 29

supermarket 17, 22, 23

trade 3

transport 3, 8–9, 16–17, 22

First published in Great Britain in 2016 by Wayland
Copyright © Wayland, 2016

All rights reserved.

Author: Michael Bright
Freelance editor: Katie Woolley
Editors: Annabel Stones and Liza Miller
Designer: Rocket Design (East Anglia) Ltd

ISBN: 9780750296458
10 9 8 7 6 5 4 3 2 1

Wayland
An imprint of
Hachette Children's Group
Part of Hodder & Stoughton
Carmelite House
50 Victoria Embankment
London EC4Y 0DZ

An Hachette UK Company
www.hachette.co.uk
www.hachettechildrens.co.uk

Printed in China

Illustrations by Stefan Chabluk: 2–3, 14

Picture credits:
All images and graphic elements courtesy of
Shutterstock except: 19br: NASA.

Every effort has been made to clear copyright.
Should there be any inadvertent omission, please
apply to the publisher for rectification.

The website addresses (URLs) included in this
book were valid at the time of going to press.
However, it is possible that contents or addresses
may have changed since the publication of this
book. No responsibility for any such changes can
be accepted by either the author or the Publisher.

The four books in the Source to Resource series examine Earth's most important resources. They support the geography curriculum and are designed to encourage readers to debate some of today's most pressing environmental issues.

FROM FIELD TO PLATE

Essential food 3
Eat up! 4
Food origins 6
In the field 8
On the farm 10
Intensive farming 12
Organic farming 14
Fresh foods 16
Preserving food 18
Friendly bugs 20
Food in shops 22
Preparing food 24
Safe food 26
World food 28

978 0 7502 9645 8

FROM OIL RIG TO PETROL PUMP

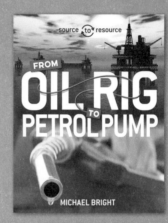

Essential oil 3
Oil 4
Oil origins 6
History of oil 8
Searching for oil 10
Extracting oil 12
Crude oil 14
Transporting crude oil 16
Oil refineries 18
Crude oil products 20
Fuel to the pump 22
Oil incidents 24
Petroleum-based products 26
Oil: the future 28

978 0 7502 9648 9

FROM RAINDROP TO TAP

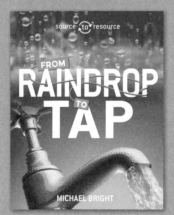

Essential water 3
The blue planet 4
The water cycle 6
Water and the weather 8
Natural water sources 10
Storing water 12
Electricity from water 14
Water treatment 16
Water for the home 18
Water at work 20
Water use in the home 22
How to save water 24
Drinking water 26
Clean water for everyone 28

978 0 7502 9650 2

FROM SUNSHINE TO LIGHT BULB

Essential Sun 3
The Sun and our Earth 4
The Sun 6
Sunlight's journey to Earth 8
Electricity from sunlight 10
Solar panels 12
Electricity reaching homes 14
Electricity use 16
Electricity in the home 18
The light bulb 20
Solar heating 22
Solar towers and furnaces 24
The future of solar energy 26
Clean energy? 28

978 0 7502 9649 6